FUNNYBALL

Observations from a
Summer at the Ballpark

BY COMEDIAN JIMMY DUNN

cartoons by Marcos Rey

Peter E. Randall Publisher LLC
Portsmouth, New Hampshire 03802
2005

Copies are available from:

www.jimmydunn.tv

published by:

Peter E. Randall Publisher LLC
Portsmouth, New Hampshire 03802
www.perpublisher.com

design:
Grace Peirce

ISBN: 1-931807-37-X

Library of Congress Control Number: 2005924423

For my dad, Bomber,

*who taught me how to throw a curveball, cast a Zebco,
and wheel a trifecta*

*and who always told me,
"Son, there are no guarantees in life, except that the
Red Sox will never win it all."*

FOREWORD

When the Red Sox won the World Series, someone said they were waiting for the other eleven signs of the Apocalypse to appear.

Here's one more: Jimmy Dunn wrote a book.

After all, Jimmy's probably only READ four or five of them in his life. And now he's an author? Miracles really do happen.

I first met Jimmy ten years ago, and have been laughing at him ever since. Or is that with him? Either way, you get the point. The man is funny. His standup is top-notch.

You'll never find a more hard-core Red Sox fan, either. Any guy who once had "dontblamebuckner" as part of his email address takes it a little too seriously, don't you think?

Jimmy spent the 2004 Red Sox season as the fan-in-the-stands/sports travel consultant for our pre-game show. His pieces were some of the funniest, most off-beat stuff we ever aired. He took on towns like Toronto, San Francisco, and New York and let Red Sox Nation know how to travel—and party—in style on the road to a championship. I'm still waiting for his travel tips on Tampa Bay, however.

Some day, his Red Sox Hawaiian shirt will probably sell for more on ebay than a World Series ring.

Chances are, you've probably read a few dozen books about the 2004 World Series by now. You've watched the DVDs. You're played back your copies of the parade. You can probably do a perfect step-by-step impersonation of Dave Roberts' Game 4 stolen base against the Yankees. Why read this book?

Because it's funny. And it's nothing like anything else you've read.

And because you'll need something to do when there's a two-hour rain delay in Arlington, Texas this July.

So sit back and enjoy. And just remember: the views expressed by Jimmy are not necessarily those of NESN, it's employees, or anyone else.

And that might be the biggest reason of all to read Funnyball.

Tom Caron
NESN Red Sox Host
May, 2005

LAS VEGAS, NEVADA

McLaren International Airport
Terminal C
Security Checkpoint

Here we go again. Over the last few months, with all the traveling I've done, I've been X-rayed more times than Evel Knievel after the Wembley jump.

The guy in front of me, a little guy, maybe five feet tall, (6'3" if you count the turban), waltzes through without raising so much as an eyebrow of suspicion from the three stooges in charge of this portal of the nation's aviational security.

I'm next. Before I even take a step toward the machine, they move in like a SWAT team.

"Sir. Step back from the machine. Step back from the machine and remove the baseball cap!"

"What?"

"You must remove your hat, sir!"

"Why?"

I've already removed my shoes, my watch, and my belt. I understand what's at stake and I'm more than willing to be reasonably cooperative, but c'mon. Take off my hat?! This guy is just busting my balls.

The head stooge (Moe, if you will) moves in for the obligatory overzealous-mall-cop explanation/lecture.

"Sir, you need to remove your hat so we can verify that you're not hiding anything underneath it."

"I'm not hiding anything? *I'm* not hiding anything?"

I can hold back no longer.

"The guy in front of me could have been smuggling a midget—you clowns didn't say boo to him."

Here comes the lecture.

"Sir, if you are referring to the gentleman wearing the turban, I should inform you that the turban is a religious article and we here at the TSA have been trained not to take any actions that would offend an individual's religious sensibilities."

This guy has no clue.

If being a Red Sox fan isn't a *religious* experience, I don't know what is!

A LITTLE BIT OF HISTORY

I make my living as a stand-up comedian.

Fifteen years ago, I started getting paid to tell stories to drunks in VFW halls, college pubs, and the back rooms of filthy Chinese restaurants.

Today, I work some of the best comedy clubs across the country, cruise ships around the world, corporate events at exclusive resorts, and the back rooms of much nicer Chinese restaurants.

Several years ago, the comedy world led me to the New England Sports Network (NESN), where I scored a gig as the co host of *Fan Attic*, a classic sports program that showed replays of the best games ever aired on the network.

I played a Boston sports fan who lived in the attic above the TV studios and was constantly digging out old tapes to watch with Boston's most diehard of fans. Anyone who knows me can attest that It wasn't exactly a brilliant piece of character acting. Even before I got the part, I *was* the Fan Attic guy.

Fan Attic was a great gig. Not only did I get to do some funny stuff on TV (my favorite being re-creating Bobby Orr's famous flying goal with the help of a shopping cart we "borrowed" from a nearby supermarket), but I also was fortunate enough to meet some of the greatest athletes in the city's history, including Orr, Cam Neely, John Bucyk, Derek Sanderson, Nomar Garciaparra, and many others. Not too many sports fans can say they sat on Rich Gedman's couch and watched a tape of the '86 Series, or threw long toss in a cow pasture on Mark Fidrich's farm.

My favorite show was the *Tough Guy Show*, (NESN didn't like my title, *Goon Summit*), a roundtable discussion on the fine art of hockey enforcement featuring Jay Miller, Chris Nilan, and Lyndon Byers. I was in heaven, surrounded by more than six thousand NHL penalty minutes.

We did about fifty *Fan Attic* shows before it ended and thanks to endless reruns the show developed a cult status with hardcore Boston sports fans. To this day, it seems every time I visit Kelley's for a roast beef sandwich, I get the "What's up, *Fan Attic* guy?" followed by some reminiscing about the Craig Neinhaus era.

After *Fan Attic*, I did some bits for *Sports Sunday*, a show on FOX hosted by my friend Butch Sterns. I was traveling a lot doing stand-up, but whenever I was in town, Butch was more than happy to have me on his show. I got away with much more there (obviously; it's FOX). I could never have interviewed Ted Williams from the door of a walk-in freezer on NESN, but we did it on FOX!

As the summer of 2004 started, I was planning the usual schedule; stand-up gigs on the Cape and Islands, a week in Vegas at the Riviera

(105 degrees on the street, but a cool 67 degrees in the sports book at Caesars), and comedy clubs around Boston.

Then the boys from NESN called again, with what turned out to be the greatest summer job anyone could possibly imagine.

FUNNYBALL

Basically, my summer job was to help make the pregame show funnier.

Baseball, balls and strikes, they had covered, with former big leaguers like Sam Horn, Jim Rice, Dennis Eckersley, and Bob Tewksbury—Guys who have been there, who know the real deal.

The daily commentary and analysis from the *Boston Globe* sportswriters is some of the best baseball insight in the game. Eric Freede's on-field reporting has you feeling as though you yourself just had lunch with the skipper. And when it comes to breaking down the nuts and bolts of a baseball game, there's nobody better at it than Jerry Remy. Period.

NESN's Tom Caron is the quintessential host for any sports discussion, knowledgeable and articulate but so down-to-earth that he'd fit right in to your local barroom argument. (Believe me, I've been there with him.)

The only thing missing from the formula was "the funny."

And while Jim Rice can probably still nail a 95 mph fastball, I'm not sure he was ever able to nail a punchline.

So I signed on to be the traveling fan: the show's correspondent from the bleachers, a big-mouthed, opinionated wise-ass in an obnoxious team-logoed Hawaiian shirt.

Travel correspondent, food critic, man on the street. Whatever it took to get a few laughs.

What follows is a series of random thoughts, ideas and observations, rantings and ravings, and nonsensical baseball babble that found its way into my notebook as I spent countless days and evenings with some of the funniest and most passionate sports fans in the world, the fans of the Boston Red Sox.

If you're looking for a game-by-game breakdown of the historic 2004 season or if you're looking for thoughtful analysis of how the Sox finally won it all, you might want to look in another book.

But if you're looking for a good argument for the implementation of midgets as major league catchers, keep reading.

ANYWHERE?!

All access to Fenway Park.

That's what the green background on the ID badge hanging around my neck signifies.

All access. Anywhere. Anytime.

If you look closely at the photo, you'll notice the awkward smirk of a guy who looks as though he just got away with something. That's because I can't believe what this woman is about to give me—a season-long, all-access pass to Fenway Park. Legit.

As she laminates, I salivate. I try to show my best poker face (although the drooling is a fairly obvious tell).

You know what people would do for this pass?!

Since I've been in the comedy business, I've scored some pretty cool perks. First-class trips to Europe. A month on a cruise ship in Tahiti. I even got to hang out backstage with Aerosmith after a private show.

But nothing compares to a season pass at Fenway Park!

I can't believe they gave me this. I can't believe I can go into Fenway anytime I want. All summer!

But wait, there's more. They're going to pay me to hang out at the ballpark with Boston fans and goof around on TV. Hundreds of thousands of Sox fans are going to see it!

"Any plans this summer?"

"Going to Fenway."

"Nice. What game?"

"All of 'em!."

A season's pass to Fenway Park! This is every Sox fan's wildest dream. I mean, besides winning the World Series, but you can't ask for everything.

Or can you?

THE PESCI POLE

"Is that the Pesci pole?" I heard her ask, in a unmistakable New York accent.

I couldn't resist.

"Yup, that's the famous Pesci pole."

"Why do they call it that?"

"Joe Pesci. The actor."

"From *Goodfellas*."

"And *My Cousin Vinny*. That's the guy."

"How come they named it after him?"

"Celebrity baseball game . . . During All-Star Weekend in '99 . . . He hit it three times."

At this point about a dozen Sox fans are listening. And fighting back the laughter.

"He plays baseball—but he's so short?"

"That's what makes him so good. Small strike zone. You gotta groove him."

The muffled laughter makes her suspicious.

"You're messing with me. Joe Pesci doesn't play baseball."

"I'm sorry. Couldn't resist. They named it the Pesci pole 'cause he paid for it. Donated it to the owners. That's all. Just playing with you. Sorry."

"I knew it. I'm not an idiot, you know. It's just my first time to Fenway."

"So you haven't seen the red seat yet?"

"What red seat?"

"The one over there in the bleachers . . . see it? That's where Santa Claus sits."

SAUSAGES

During one early summer evening at Fenway, I was standing in the concession line when I overheard the following conversation between two Sox fans.

"I'm getting a sausage. You want one?"

"Sausage? No way. They'll kill ya. You know how bad those things are for your heart?"

The irony of this statement hit me quicker than Nomar swinging at the first pitch.

Here we were, getting ready to watch a team that has been tearing out hearts across New England for close to a century now, and this guy's worried about the coronary repercussions of a sausage sandwich.

That evening, as I watched the game from the right-field roof, I wrote in my notebook an homage to the greatest of all ballpark foods, the sausage.

There is nothing more enticing to a baseball fan than the smell of a freshly grilled sausage.

If you could bottle that aroma, you'd put Estée Lauder out of business. Forget the White Diamonds, ladies. You wanna attract us? Try a little Eau de Sausage!

Lately it seems as though every health freak on the planet is trying to kill my sausage buzz by telling me how unhealthy they are. We've all got that friend, right? The born-again fat guy who was about a week away from a pine-box nap, but now thinks he's Lance Armstrong because the wife has him peddling his bicycle to the mailbox instead of the SUV.

Leave me alone, Dr. Phil! I'm having a sausage!

And none of that new-age chicken-apple-tofu crap either. I'm talking *real* sausage. Made from *real* dead pigs. And *real* dead-pig by-products.

My favorite health-nut-spewed, anti-sausage propaganda?

"You know those things are bad for your heart, right?"

My heart? My heart?!

I'm a diehard Red Sox fan. You think a sausage is gonna hurt my heart?

In '78, my barely developed heart was irreparably damaged when it was smashed over the Green Monster by a guy with a corked bat and warning-track power.

In '86, my heart was marinated like a meatball by Bob Stanley and Calvin Schiraldi kicked around the infield dirt for a while, before finally being served up on a bed of right-field lawn.

And in '03, during game 7, my heart literally stopped when Grady left the mound *without* Pedro.

I think it was the nitrates in the sausage that finally kicked my heart back to life.

Point is, my heart is surrounded by more baseball scar tissue than Tim Wakefield's knuckles. And you health nuts think you're gonna fix that by stuffing my sausage with tofu?

The following afternoon we shot a piece for the show in the shadow of the Green Monster on Landsdowne Street with the help of my friend "the Sausage Guy," a Boston institution, purveyor of late-night munchies for the Fenway faithful. The Sausage Guy has cooked more late-night snacks for hungry drunks than the George Foreman grill in John Daily's Winnebago.

I worked the spatula and the lunch crowd as I ranted and raved about the virtues of the sausage sandwich.

The bit was a hit and it ran on the pregame show and a bunch of times on *Red Sox Rewind*. Within a few days, the nods of recognition from Sox fans at Fenway were accompanied by a "What's up, sausage guy?" I had no idea that this three minutes of comedy material was going to result in dozens of fans insisting to buy me sausage sandwiches in the months to come.

In retrospect, I should have written a bit about how much I love twenty-dollar bills or '65 Mustangs.

THE FINE ART OF BODY PAINT

Sure, you can always support your favorite big leaguer by dropping two hundred bucks for an authentic jersey with his name of the back and wearing it proudly to the ballpark.

But nothing says commitment to the team more than half a dozen fat guys using their bellies as a human billboard.

Here are some tips on how to do it right, from a guy who has painted his chest on more than a few occasions.

Choosing the Right Paint

Most fans figure a quick trip to the local hardware store should do the trick.

"Something in a bright red."

"Interior or exterior?"

"Definitely exterior."

Yes, the gallon of Benjamin Moore house paint will certainly be more than enough to paint you and a handful of your drunken buddies, but you'll need a sandblaster and a gallon of turpentine to get that stuff off once you sober up, rookie.

The experienced parking-lot Picasso gets his body-paint supplies at the local art store.

Water-based. kid-safe. Ages three and up.

Just because it says FINGER PAINT on the can doesn't mean you can't dip a brush in it and apply it liberally to your giant belly.

Body Typing

Don't make the fattest guy the O. Too easy! It's much funnier to make him the *I* and the 90 pound weakling the *O*.

Keep It Simple

Four guys spelling out T-R-O-T is a pretty easy task.

M-I-E-N-T-K-I-E-W-I-C-Z is a bit more ambitious.

Years ago, my brother and I came to blows in a drunken argument over how many P's are in Hipolito.

This brings us to another important point: spelling.

Always designate a sober person to spell-check.

And stay together.

Five guys in the bleachers spelling out M-A-N-N-Y look pretty cool. But if the M and the Y make a beer run, you've got three morons cheering on A-N-N.

And if you're the Y and you wander away from the group, you'll get a million dickheads asking you, "Why not?"

Clean Up

Go to bed drunk with a big red letter painted to your chest and you're bound to ruin a good set of sheets. You'll sweat out the booze, it'll cause the paint to run, and your bedroom will look like a *Soprano's* crime scene.

Instead, stop at the self-serve car wash on the way home. Line up the crew against the wall and hose 'em down like incoming prisoners at the delousing station.

THE HUMAN BILLBOARD

Here's a body-paint stunt I've wanted to execute, but haven't been able to put together logistically. Maybe you can.

It was inspired by the rotating billboards that have become so prevalent at the ballpark.

Travel to enemy territory.

Preferably the Bronx.

You'll need six co-conspirators, minimum.

In the parking lot, paint one letter on each of your friends' chests, spelling out Y-A-N-K-E-E-S.

Line them up for a dry run, then on their backs, paint "S-U-C-K".

The extra bodies get exclamation points. For emphasis!

Put your shirts back on and enjoy the game.

Timing is critical. Wait for the end of an inning and disrobe.

Watch the cameras. They'll be looking for you. They always try to show some interesting fans when the broadcast returns from commercial break.

Designate a captain to call the turn. On his signal, make Vanna White proud.

If well executed, the commentary will go something along the lines of . . .

"Some very proud Yankees fans showing their alliegiance, . . . No, wait a second, check that. Looks like some very creative Red Sox fans."

Then run like hell.

LOOKED LIKE A STRIKE FROM HERE!

If you're a major-league ball player, arguing balls and strikes can cost you $250. That's some serious coin for a guy who's only making eight or nine million a year. Remember, these guys need to feed their families.

Fortunately, for the gang in the bleachers, MLB has yet to begin fining fans for the same offense.

Without a doubt, my favorite comment from the stands is "Looked like a strike from here!"

I just wish the guy would finish his statement with full disclosure.

"Looked like a strike from here . . . twenty-six rows back in the bleachers, some six hundred feet away from the strike zone, where I've been sitting for the last three hours while I fired down God-knows-how-many beers. Sure my vision is slightly blurred by the sunblock that I got

in my left eye while adjusting my contact, and admittedly my view is obstructed by the guy in front of me with the Cosmo Kramer hairdo, and to be 100 percent honest, I was only watching the game with one eye, the other being permanently fixated on the redheaded coed from B.U. in the skimpy bikini top with the sun-soaked, glistening breasts . . .

But it looked like a strike from here!

THE GREEN LINE

To get the real Boston fan experience, you need to take a game-day ride to Fenway on the Green Line, North America's oldest operating subway system. The word operating is used very loosely here. The Green Line trains break down more often than Ken Griffey Jr.

The brutal humidity of midsummer subterranean Boston is offset by the ice-cold air conditioners that work properly about one day a month. The rest of the summer—aromatherapy for baseball fans: an odor combination of alcohol, sunblock, and B.O. that if emitted from a candle at some fancy boutique at the mall would be called Green Line Gross.

But for sheer thrill-ride value, the Green Line simply can't be beat.

Superman Ride of Steel at Six Flags Amusement Park—two hours from Boston and thirty-five dollars to get in.

Green Line token—a buck and a quarter.

Sudden turns, screeching stops for no apparent reason, erratic acceleration—close your eyes and you'd swear you were riding shotgun in Jose Conseco's Ferrari.

On game day, Sox fans are jammed into these trains like cattle, fighting with rush-hour commuters for handrails like kids playing Twister. Bill Lambier would admire the elbow work. Through the intercom system, conductors yell at the claustrophobic passengers to pack in even closer or he "ain't closin' the door!" Boarding becomes an every-man-for-himself drill, a clinic in incivility.

The rare empty seat looks tempting, but don't make the rookie mistake, especially on the way home! The last place you want your head to be is ass level on a train full of baseball fans who have been drinking beer and eating hot dogs and nachos all night.

The ride in to Fenway is somewhat more civilized, comparatively speaking. Optimism, enthusiasm, and relative sobriety. Fans discuss starting pitchers' ERAs, Trot's trouble with lefties and how Tek needs to come out of his slump soon.

The ride out is a frat party on rails, especially after a big win! No discussions, no debates. Just a forty-five-minute chorus of "YANKEES SUCK! . . . YANKEES SUCK! . . . YANKEES SUCK!"

The most celebrated ride on the Green Line was taken on Marathon Monday 1980, by a woman named Rosie Ruiz. Rosie decided that rather than running the grueling 26.2-mile course, she would opt for public transportation. She hopped on the Green Line, jumped out near the finish in Fenway, and jogged in for the win.

Her fellow runners got suspicious when they noticed that Rosie had barely broken a sweat.

Just her luck. The one day she rides the green line, the air conditioner was working. What are the odds?

WALLY'S GOONS

Whenever Wally, the Green Monster, makes a public appearance, he's constantly flanked by a couple of guys wearing shirts that read SECURITY across the back.

That's a sad statement on the times when a ballpark mascot needs Secret Service.

And it can't be the proudest of moments when you must admit that your occupation is "puppet protection."

OVERHEARD AT THE PARK

"What do you do with the skin on the nuts?" asked a young woman who was obviously experiencing her first bag of ball-park peanuts.

To which a fan from the crowd replied, "Tickle it with your finger-nails!"

WINDOW SHOPPING IN NYC

Saw a cool shirt in the window of Saks Fifth Avenue today, so I went
inside to see how much it cost.

Four hundred dollars.

A Four hundred dollar shirt!

I wouldn't buy a Four hundred dollar shirt if Fred Lynn played in it
and Ginger Lynn was wearing it.

VITAMIN S

Jason Giambi's not playing today. Has a stomach virus.

Is that what they're calling the Balco flu these days?

Look, it's no secret who's juicing up. One year a guy's a string bean and the next season he shows up at camp looking like Popeye.

As long as there has been competition, there has been someone looking to cheat. And if these idiots want to destroy their own bodies with steroids, good luck to 'em.

Personally, I think a steroid-free game, if it ever happens, is going to be more boring than a Meg Ryan–Tom Hanks movie.

I'm a big fan of power. Wade Boggs bored me. Mark McGwire mesmerized me.

Be careful what you wish for: no juice = no jacks.

I'd much rather a league full of Frankensteins than a league full of David Ecksteins.

Even the baseball purists, the ones who say that this steroid era is tainting the game, will be the first to complain when halfway through the season, Rocco Baldelli is leading the league in homers . . . with eight.

I say give 'em all the needles they want. I dread the day of the juice-free league. And so will you.

If I want to see a bunch of little people running around a field and not scoring, I'll start watching soccer.

HELL

After spending a few days in New York City, with the Yankees enjoying an eight-game lead over my Sox, it occurred to me that this is probably what hell is going to be like.

I'm absolutely certain that when I arrive in hell (Let's face it, I'm in—first ballot) the devil will be wearing a Yankees hat. A special retro-fitted lid with little holes cut out for his horns. I can just picture him, babbling on his Nextel (the annoying walkie-talkie one) with Stein-brenner on the other end, talking shop.

That's what I expect to find in hell, millions of Yankees fans, and I expect them to torment me for eternity.

It'll be hot, sticky, and smelly all the time, like an August garbage day in the Bronx. And I'll spend my days watching Yankee highlights from the YES network on a beautiful sixty inch high-definition TV. The video—perfect. The audio will be edited so the only voice I can hear is that of Tim McCarver.

And they never let me sleep, like a baseball version of the Chinese water torture. Just when I start to nod off, Billy Martin whacks me in the shins with a fungo bat and Phil Rizutto yells in my ear, "Holy cow!"

Boggs is there. So is Clemens. They laugh at me—like they knew the whole time.

Just when I think the afterlife can get no worse, Billy Crystal walks by and promises that after dinner (Manhattan clam chowder) he'll be treating us to some fireplace stories about the Mick.

I need to repent. Now.

SUCKER PUNCH

I was punched by a Yankees fan today. Seems about right, huh?

Let me tell ya something, this chick was tough.

I'm not joking. A "lady" in a Yankees shirt flipped me off and then punched me in the chest as the Yankees finally finished off the Sox in fourteen innings. (one of the greatest baseball games I've ever seen in person, the outcome notwithstanding).

I had tried to keep a low profile as I watched from the loge, but it was difficult to hide my allegiance as I was wearing my work clothes, specifically my Red Sox Hawaiian shirt.

When the Sox made the final out, the New York fans celebrated, and part of the celebration included this woman flipping me off.

I snapped a quick photo of her (a Kodak moment for sure), and she responded by punching me in the chest.

"Who are you, Sean Penn?"

So much for "fan-friendly environment".

I might have fought back, but I was seriously afraid of her. You would have been, too.

As Sinatra sang over the stadium speakers "I want to be a part of it, New York, New York!" I thought for a moment I heard him say, "Hey kid, get the hell out of here. You don't wanna mess with this broad!"

THIRD PERSON

I am so sick of listening to these self-important athletes talk about themselves in the third person. I promise you this, no matter how famous I become, you'll never hear Jimmy Dunn talking like that.

TOMMY JOHN SURGERY

You have to feel for Tommy John. Here's a guy who played for twenty-six years in the bigs, won nearly three hundred games, a four-time All-Star . . .

And what is he remembered for? Elbow surgery.

That can't be very comforting when you are about to go under the knife and they say, "We haven't really decided what to call this medical procedure yet, but if it works, we're thinking about naming it after you."

I guess there's *one* thing worse than having a surgery named after you, however, and that's getting your own disease.

I'm sure Lou Gehrig would have traded all his problems in a second for a bum elbow.

RACIAL KARAOKE

The public address announcement made at Yankee Stadium regarding racial and ethnic slurs was not unlike the many announcements encouraging a   fan-friendly, politically correct environment at ballparks across the country.

Then, seconds later, they blasted a song called "Black Betty."

You know the tune. We all know it. We've been singing along to it for years.

It's a song about Black Betty. Wham a lam. Who had a child. Wham a lam. And the damn thing went wild.

Remember, fans, no racial slurs.

Now, sing along with us about the wild bastard child from Alabama.

"WHOA . . . BLACK BETTY . . . WHOA . . . BLACK BETTY! . . . WHAM A LAM!"

MY REPUTATION PRECEDES ME

Stepping out of a cab in downtown San Francisco, and the Sox fans are already here in mass (pun intended).

No more than thirty seconds passes when a guy sticks his head out the side of a rental Mustang, points at me and yells, "SAUSAGE GUY!"

Not the city in which you want to have that nickname.

SAN FRANCISCO

I've been into kayaking for years, and have paddled in some of the coolest places in the world. I've paddled a kayak alongside one-hundred-foot yachts in the Caribbean. I've paddled for days with drunken college buddies down the Saco River in Maine. I've paddled recklessly down the face of a twenty-foot wave in Tahiti and shortly thereafter desperately across a dry reef. But without a doubt, the coolest waterway I've ever navigated is McCovey Cove in San Francisco.

From the first time I saw some idiot on TV sitting in that harbor, chasing baseballs with a butterfly net, I knew that some day, I would be that idiot.

Inter-league play, in my opinion, is a wonderful thing, for many reasons, but mostly because it encourages fans to travel to new cities. And from the first day I saw the Sox schedule last spring, I had this weekend circled for a kayak trip.

I found a rental shop online and made a reservation for a three-hour tour.

For safety reasons, I was required to wear the tourist issue bright orange life jacket, at least until I paddled out of the view of the rental shop. But with so many Giants fans in the harbor and so many Boston fans on the dock, I wanted everyone to see my Sox shirt, so my flotation devise quickly became my seat cushion.

The water in McCovey Cove reminds me of Mexico. Not the crystal clear, turquoise-tinted ocean off the shores of Cabo San Lucas, but the water in the toilets in the nightclubs in Tijuana during spring break. I immediately decided I was not going to dive after a Barry Bonds home run if it meant rushing to the hospital for a tetanus shot. If I catch a ball, it's gonna have to be hit right at me. Today, I play the outfield like Dante Bichette, not Dewey Evans.

The harbor was littered with every type of floating vessel imaginable. I saw a family picnicking on the deck of a forty-foot sailboat, grilling steak and shrimp and sipping wine from fine stemware. Anchored next to them, I saw two guys in a life raft, who looked as though they may have just escaped from Alcatraz, splitting a twelve-pack of Coors. There were kayaks, canoes, rowboats, rubber rafts, speedboats, sailboats, and a guy in an inflatable children's swimming pool.

Two fans in the water were clearly pros—Alligator Man and the Kayak Man.

Alligator Man paddles the cove on a regular basis, but has yet to bring in a coveted Bonds "splash hit." He is a very sociable guy—in fact he even offered me a cold beverage, which I quickly accepted. The seven foot inflatable alligator bungeed to the front of his kayak may intimidate paddlers, but once you talk to him for a few minutes, you realize he's just out there to have fun, and if a ball comes his way, it's a bonus.

Kayak Man is all business. And he's got the numbers to prove it. He wears a t-shirt listing his numerous catches and his web address when he hears Bonds' name on his portable radio, he snaps to full attention.

Everyone in the water quickly realizes that Barry is at bat, and all eyes turn to the sky, as the water churns with anticipating strokes of the paddles.

But Pedro Martinez is on the hill today, so the Alligator Man will go away empty netted once again.

In fact, on this afternoon, only one ball made it out of the park, a loud foul that was grabbed by a quick-handed fan on the dock before it was able to splash.

I did make one successful grab, however, scoring a basket of garlic fries from a guy named Joe who runs a delivery service from the dock by way of a fishing rod attached to a bucket. For a small convenience fee,

Joe will run to the nearby concession window and get you some delicious ballpark cuisine and lower it right onto the deck of your vessel.

As I paddled back along the wharf, I was cheered by some of the many Sox fans who were in San Francisco. Despite all the traffic in McCovey Cove on this particular afternoon, I was the only Boston fan in the flotilla.

Someday, I thought as I docked, I hope to navigate these waterways again, and I hope to catch my first splash ball, a towering home run off the bat of David Ortiz, in the ninth inning of game 7 of the World Series.

VOLUNTARY TESTING

Amid the ongoing accusations of steroid use, Barry Bonds continues to tell the press he's willing to "pee in a cup."

It's no big deal, Barry. I know guys in the bleachers who have been peeing in cups for years.

On the field at Camden Yards, getting ready to "bring the funny." T.C. is talking to me into that earpiece reminding me not to screw up.

In the Bronx with a little protection from New York's Finest.

Some friendly faces in enemy territory.

My summer office at Fenway.

The infamous notebook.

The boys on the roof.

Paying a little "visit" to the Yanks pro shop.

Skydome. Good seats still available.

MIDGET CATCHERS

Baseball teams have long been weary of signing aging catchers to long-term contracts, fearing the inevitable physical breakdown that comes with years of playing the grueling position.

The problem lies in the crouch. The human body just isn't designed to endure the constant up and down.

Well, most human bodies.

But what about midgets?

A midget would be able to stand erect behind the plate and still place his mitt comfortably in the strike zone.

No bending. No back stress. No sore knees.

He may have a bit of a challenge reaching up for the high cheese, but that's a small price to pay for longevity.

It's high time that baseball looks into the concept of the midget catcher.

They've certainly proved their athletic prowess in other sports (see: midget wrestling; Sky Low Low, inch for inch, was one of the greatest athletes ever).

They've proved extremely durable (see: dwarf tossing).

And their equipment would be cheap because they'd fit into children's sizes.

Critics will say the use of midgets as catchers would be unfairly exploiting the little people. I say quite the contrary.

The job openings in baseball would give midgets an opportunity to get involved in the entertainment industry without being subject to the humiliation of working in an Austin Powers movie or novelty porn.

I say it's time for some brave general manager to cast aside his conception of the prototypical catcher and prove himself a bigger man, by giving a little guy a chance to throw on the tools of ignorance.

DITKA

Met a football legend at the baseball park today. The last person I expected to see watching B.P. at Fenway was Mike Ditka, but there he was, sitting all by himself.

I couldn't resist the opportunity to meet Mike Ditka, despite the fact that he was clearly enjoying his privacy. Sucks to be famous.

I walked right up to him, introduced myself, and immediately froze.

There were a hundred question's spinning around in my head.

"How's that Ricky Williams trade looking now?"

"Ever see the Fridge?"

"Does that Levitra stuff really work?"

But the best I could come up with was, "Here for the game?"

Brilliant.

What a moron I am. A chance to pick the mind of a football genius, and I ask him, "Here for the game?"

You know Ditka's thinking, "No I'm here for an oil change, you idiot."

But he obviously sensed the awkwardness, and was probably a bit concerned about the presence of this nervous nut in the ridiculous Hawaiian shirt who may or may not have snuck into Fenway, so he quickly deflected.

"Yup, here for the game. Nice to meet you, Jimmy Dunn."

Dismissed.

"Nice to meet you, coach. Say hi to the Fridge for me."

22-0

Out-of-Town Scores

September 1, 2004

The Yankees lost to Cleveland last night, 22-0.

22-0!

I haven't felt this good since I heard my ex-girlfriend was making adult videos!

And the same question begs to be asked.

"Anyone know where I can get a tape?"

MEMO TO ALL CATCHERS

If you strike out the pitcher, please refrain from throwing the ball around the horn.

You just struck out the pitcher.

If it took more than three pitches, you should be ashamed.

It was the pitcher.

He's hitting .132.

Thank God I don't live in a National League city. Think about how much time they waste retiring pitchers and then celebrating the feat.

I'm such a huge fan of the DH that I actually believe each team should have two designated hitters: one for the pitcher—and one for the second baseman.

SERVICE WITH A SMILE

I'm constantly amazed by the rude treatment some of the privileged fans in the roof box seats impose on their servers. I just don't get it. A guy is gonna go in the other room, pour a beverage into a cup—a beverage that you will then drink—and you're gonna be a dick to him . . . *before he gets the drink!*

You're either very confident that he will be a professional server, despite your demeanor (a tall order considering he's only making six bucks an hour to take your crap), or incredibly naive.

Because if I was getting that drink, you be sampling the newest microbrew on the market . . . a nice cold mug of *salty nut draft.*

CHEW

Despite the fact that everyone knows the health risks associated with chewing tobacco, it's still incredibly popular with baseball players . . . *and baseball fans.*

Today a guy at Fenway offered me a pinch and when I declined the generous offer he said, "It's Skoal apple long-cut. Tastes just like a Jolly Rancher!"

Well, in that case, . . . gimme a coupla fingers.

Sure, the surgeon general has determined that chewing tobacco causes oral cancer, gum disease, ulcerative colitis, and leukoplakic lesions, but if it tastes like a Jolly Rancher . . . well, I'd risk all that to get me the taste of a Jolly Rancher.

Call me a health nut if you will, but when I want the taste of a Jolly Rancher, I have . . . a Jolly Rancher.

And if I'm really craving a mouthful of chewy, apple-flavored, deliciousness, you know what also works?

An apple.

POKER FACE

I was enjoying a sandwich and watching the fans leave Fenway from my usual spot on the corner of Landsdowne when I noticed a familiar face in the crowd, that of poker pro Phil Helmuth.

I introduced myself and told him I'd see him at a card table sometime soon.

He told me he hears that often.

I invited him to play in our weekly comedians game while he was in town, but he graciously declined.

Too bad.

I would have loved to see the look on his face when Frank asks, for the third time in twenty minutes, which is better, three of a kind or a flush.

A COUPLE OF DOGS, A COLD BEER, AND A QUICK CREDIT CHECK

"*PSST!* Have I got a deal for you!"

"Sign up today for a credit card and get a free towel with your favorite team's logo."

Well, I was just headed to take a leak while they bring in the relief pitcher, but sure, why not take a few minutes for some financial planning.

"Does it have an annual fee?"

"Nope. Just a minimal yearly convenience charge."

"What's the interest rate?"

"It's based on prime."

"So it's prime?"

"Based on prime . . . plus your age."

"Late fees?"

"Only when you're late."

"And I get this free towel today?"

"And the key chain!"

"You gotta be an idiot to turn down this deal! Sign me up!"

"OK, I just need you to fill out this brief forty-three-page document in triplicate . . ."

* Legal Disclaimer *

This conversation and/or transaction never actually happened. It's fictitious. In fact, It's not even close to the wonderful deals the fine folks in the banking industry regularly offer the inebriated patrons of sporting events around the country.

BALTIMORE

The road trip to Camden Yards is always a popular one with Sox fans. This particular trip just happen to coincide with the big Democratic National Convention in Boston, so as our fine city prepared to host John Kerry and his supporters, the residents of Boston fled to Baltimore.

Logan Airport was a bizarre scene: Sox fans heading out, politicians heading in.

"Afternoon, Govna, lock up the city when you're done with it. Vote Quimby!"

For weeks leading up to the DNC, Boston's residents were warned of traffic problems and security issues that were going to make living in the city a nightmare. Many took the warning, donned their Pedro shirts, and headed south.

Baltimore is an ideal road-trip city.

The park, malls, hotels, and restaurants are located in the same waterfront area. Tickets are readily available (although the upper deck is higher than Darryl Strawberry with a key to Gotham!). And Camden Yards is still one of the best ballparks in baseball.

Best Heckle Heard at Camden Yards

Dude, it's gotta suck being in a bird costume for a living, and you're not even on *Sesame Street!*

BOOG'S BBQ

No trip to Camden Yards is complete without a trip to Boog's. A bear of a man, with a giant head and a giant smile, Boog actually sits at the bar and joyfully poses for photos with fans. He looks like John Candy in the *Blues Brothers* so much that I was waiting for him to order me up an Orange Whip.

And here's a surprise—the food is *great!* The best food I've ever had at a ballpark. Ever.

These days it's become trendy to have ex big leaguers put their name on concession stands. At Fenway, El Tiante's Cubano sandwiches are very popular and the new Rem Dawgs were an instant hit. Why stop there? Why not turn all of Yawkee way into a giant big league buffet.

I can here the vendor barking now . . .

"C'mon down to the Yawkee Way Big League Buffet! Step right up to the plate and savor some of the finest ex-ballplayer-endorsed cuisine anywhere.

"Just looking to snack? Then grab yourself a bag of Pedro Astacio pistachios.

"Want Something more substantial? How 'bout a nice Todd Benzinger burger? Or visit Rick Burleson's and watch the Rooster slow cook some bird over Smoky Joe wood.

In the mood for Italian? Try a Frank Malzone calzone or a plate of Rick Lancellotti manicotti, with a couple of big ol' Bob Stanley meatballs!

Dieting? Don't worry. At Bernie Low Carbo's we've got you covered with a bowl of Pumpsie Greens or a nice Eric Wedge of lettuce. Or for a very limited time, try our Cesar Crespo.

"Wash down the whole meal with a nice cold Oil Can at the Denny Galehouse Alehouse where we have a wide assortment of brew as well as a vintage Carl Everett wine.

"So eat up at the Yawkee Way Big League Buffet! But please, go easy. We don't want to take you out of here in the Bruce Hurst."

REASONS TO VISIT TAMPA BAY

TORONTO

I think it's kinda cute how the border guards in Canada make it seem as though you're entering another country.

OK, technically Canada *is* another country, but let's face it: if we wanted Canada, it would be our fifty-first state tomorrow.

Believe me, the day a scientist discovers a way to power an internal combustion engine with maple syrup, the American-Canadian War is on.

War? OK, minor skirmish.

We wouldn't even need our military. We could just send up Kid Rock and a few of his Bad-Ass boys from Detroit Rock City for the weekend and they'd bring home the entire Canadian mounted patrol in the trunk of a Cadillac Eldorado.

Fortunately for the Canadians, on this trip north we Americans come in peace. I've joined thousands of Sox fans on a baseball pilgrimage to the house that Joe Carter built for some good old-fashioned baseball fun.

Toronto is a another great trip for Sox fans for many reasons.

Number one: Tickets!

Fenway seats are like gold these days, and every day they get more and more difficult for the average fan to obtain. Not the case in Toronto. They're giving 'em away! You can walk up to the window two minutes before game time and pick your seat. It's even more fun to buy tickets from scalpers, because it's a buyer's market.

And there is no satisfaction greater than that which comes from screwing a scalper!

TORONTO TRAVEL TIP: Skydome

Make sure to get a level-one ticket. The real cheap level-two and -three sections are cordoned off, and despite the fact that hundreds of level-one seats are vacant, the ushers won't let you down the stairs. (If you really get stuck upstairs, sneak into the elevator and fake a lost-child emergency.)

Number two: Exchange rate!

Canadian currency is a joke. Just look at it. Our money has pictures of distinguished-looking former presidents. Canadian bills have poems about why they love hockey.

Turn your dead presidents into hockey haikus and the relative cost of a lap dance is about four bucks!

TORONTO TRAVEL TIP

The Strip House is a steak joint. The establishment you're really looking for is called the Brass Rail. It's on Yonge street. (I was well into a $28 sirloin before I realized there would be no live nude girls—or baked potato.)

⚾

Number three: Road trip!

What could be more fun than packing up the whole Grisworld clan in the wagon and driving eight hours to another country for a ball game? Don't forget Nana.

Once you get there, you can park the car for the weekend. There are dozens of hotels right next to the park, and everything is within walking (or staggering) distance.

⚾

TORONTO TRAVEL TIP

Identification

You'd think that in this age of international terrorism you'd need certain documentation to get into a foreign country, but all you need to get into Canada is a picture ID. I used a Mike Greenwell '88 Topps card.

⚾

Skydome

The Toronto Skydome is a soulless cement bunker, a field of concrete.

I imagine the inspiration came to the design team from a voice that said, "If you mix it, they will come."

Cover the field with some of the ugliest Astroturf imaginable, stuff you'd put on the front porch of a Kentucky mobile home, and it looks like they're playing baseball on a barroom pool table.

THE THREE GREATEST MOMENTS AT SKYDOME

3. Joe Carter's dramatic World Series—winning home run off Mitch "Wild Thing" Williams.

2. When Dave Winfield killed the seagull with a baseball. (Billy Martin later said it was the first time he hit the cutoff man all year.)

1. The night a couple was caught having sex in the hotel room that overlooked the game.

The hotel rooms at Skydome offer a unique place to watch a ball game. They also offer a unique place for the hardcore baseball fan to get one's swerve on.

Strictly in the name of research for this book, I decided to try and reenact the infamous amorous evening.

I figured that with the right timing and the right lighting, there was no way the TV cameras could ignore an intimate interlude in the middle of a boring Blue Jays game.

There were two problems.

One—a willing co-conspirator.

Two—the right room.

I decided to solve the woman problem with an inflatable companion, readily available at any of the abundant sex shops conveniently located in the downtown shopping area.

Now all I needed was the right room.

I went to the hotel desk and inquired about the availability of the "winner's suite." Unfortunately, it was booked.

Later in the day I tried to return my "date," but for some reason the store has a no-return policy on blow up sex toys.

TORONTO TRAVEL TIP:
Another Cool Way to Watch the Game

The Hard Rock has plenty of window seats with great views of the game and no ticket is required, only a minimum food order. Call ahead. They take reservations up to two months in advance, and unlike the seats below, these will sell out.

WAYNE GRETZKY'S

What sports fan wouldn't want to have lunch at a restaurant named after the greatest hockey player of all time and themed to honor his Hall of Fame career?

Unfortunately, Bobby Orr doesn't have a restaurant, so you'll have to settle for Wayne Gretzky's. It's right around the corner from Skydome, a favorite hangout for sports fans before and after the game.

I ordered the Nachos 99 and a Great One Burger and took a stroll around the restaurant/museum. I asked the bartender/curator where the Jay Miller wing was and he had no idea who I was talking about.

That's gratitude. Jay protected Gretzky's skinny ass for years in L.A., fighting off goon after goon, and he doesn't get so much as a salad named after him.

After eating my lunch and talking junior hockey with a guy at the bar for a while, I paid my check, left a tip for the busboy (who looked an awful lot like Jarri Kurri) and went in the men's room and dropped a Dominic Hasek.

THE HOCKEY HALL OF FAME

After my lunch at Gretzky's, I walked a few blocks and found my way to the Hockey Hall of Fame.

Its exhibit on the Old Boston Garden was less than impressive. Honestly, I have more authentic Garden stuff in my living room.

But what was impressive was the Great Hall, home to all the trophies I had dreamed of hoisting overhead as a kid (except the Lady Byng—*nobody* wants to win that one).

After being assured that the Stanley Cup on display was indeed a replica, I posed for a photo opportunity. I had to be absolutely certain it wasn't the real thing, as we all know that touching the Cup before you win it is bad luck, and despite the fact that I'm in my thirties and still can't skate backwards very well, I'm still holding out hope. Hey, if the Tampa Bay Lightning can win it, I gotta have an outside shot.

Finally, before leaving the Hall of Fame, there was one more thing I had to do. I visited the men's room and took another Dominic Hasek.

THE CN TOWER

Located right next to Skydome, the CN Tower stands over 1,500 feet tall. If you go to the top, you can actually see parts of the United States. This proves how boring life in Canada actually is; they built this tower just so they could see us doing something.

Fortunately, the baseball fans of Canada aren't nearly as passionate as Sox fans. If our team was twenty-nine games out of first place in August, they'd certainly have to close the 1,500 foot "observation deck" adjacent to the ballpark.

Leaving Canada

Upon returning to U.S. soil, when asked if you have anything to declare, the incorrect answer is "Yeah, the Blue Jays blow!"

A FAN TAKES A SEAT . . .
TO THE HEAD!

September 14, 2004

I spent a low-key evening at Fenway up on the right-field roof with another comedian, my friend Rich Ceisler. We watched a rookie from Tampa Bay pitch a hell of a game against the Sox and eventually beat Pedro Martinez.

Just another night on the roof. Couple of steak-tip subs, social visit from Big Sam Horn. Fenway fall.

But the big baseball story of the day was out of Oakland, where a woman fan was hit with a folding chair thrown by Texas Rangers pitcher Frank Francisco, a response to some verbal abuse the Rangers pitching staff received from the Oakland crowd.

A perfectly acceptable response to some mean-spirited heckling, right? These boisterous fans got exactly what they deserved . . . an old school WWF folding-chair-o-gram. You hurt our feelings, we hurt your wife.

Major League Baseball says it is investigating the incident. The only thing it should be investigating is what day on the A's upcoming schedule is available for Throw-a-Chair-at-Frank-Francisco Day.

Tie him to the backstop and let the fun begin. One by one, fans get to give Frank an overdose of his own medicine. "MLB's Fan Furniture Toss. Brought to you by Ethan Allen." I live for this!

This guy Francisco should be banned for life, shunned so far away from the game that he needs to call Pete Rose to get his baseball news.

Francisco was booked that evening on felony assault and posted bond. And the woman was on TV the next day, with a lawyer, a taped-up nose, and a couple of shiners, looking like she just said "Make your own damn dinner" to Ike Turner.

Just days after the Kobe show was canceled, Court TV got its new fall schedule.

On my way home I listened to the overnight radio guy pontificate about obnoxious sports fans and how their heckling can cross the line and how their attitude caused this altercation. What?!

It was the fans' fault? You can't be serious!

Look, if there is anyone who knows about heckling it's me.

In my fifteen years in the comedy business, I've been heckled more than any relief pitcher in baseball history. I've been heckled by drunks, jerks, friends, friends who are drunks, drunks who are friends, drunk friends who are jerks, husbands, wives, college students, bankers, truckers, bikers, carpenters, scientists, the entire Weymouth Air Force Base, and once, at a fund-raising event, by ex-Sox reliever Bob Stanley (who, incidentally, responded to my rebuttal by pretending to toss a chair at *me*).

Maybe I'm missing something here, But I'm not sure there is anything that someone could *say* to me that would justify responding with
a flying chair to the noggin.

Oh, believe me, if it was legally acceptable to toss chairs when
assaulted with insults, I'd have moved more furniture than Barry and
Eliot!

But to say this was the fans' fault is just asinine!

CSI FENWAY

I was socializing with one of my usher friends at Fenway when a fan who had clearly been drinking for some time, approached with an alarmed look on his face.

"Man, I don't want to freak anybody out, but over in the garage, there's a couple of bodies lying in the corner."

The guy was right . . . kind of.

The Farrelly brothers were using Fenway after hours to shoot *Fever Pitch* and one of the Hollywood tricks they employ when shooting stadium scenes is to use inflatable dummies as extras. While it was obvious to the sober eye that the bodies in question were, in fact, inflatables, the prop department would be proud in the knowledge that they had this guy fooled.

DRUNKEN SCOREBOARD WATCHING

"So the Sox are four and a half back and they're winning tonight. How are the Yankees doing tonight?"

—overheard at Fenway, while the Sox were winning . . . against the Yankees.

SWEEP

With the Sox up two games to none over the Angels, you know this is pretty much over and it's just a matter of time before we inevitably square off with the Yankees, right? (Assuming they hold up their end of the deal and take care of the resilient Twins.)

But I thought it was still a bit premature for the celebration I encountered under the grandstands, shortly after the start of game 3 at Fenway.

There I found a group of drunken fans circling a man with a broom chanting, "Sweep! Sweep! Sweep!"

Here's the best part. The guy with the broom wasn't a clever fan rubbing in the series' impending results with a funny prop.

He was a janitor.

AND SO IS YOUR WIFE!

Outside Fenway today, after game 4 of the ALCS, I saw a guy proudly marching around while carrying my favorite sign of the season. It read, MATSUI IS UGLY!

JIMMY KIMMEL LIVE

Due to some poor planning on my part, the comedy business took me out to Chicago for an afternoon gig entertaining a banquet of jubilant accountants. Nothing more exciting than a lunchtime show for a ballroom full of number-crunchers. No business like show business.

Game 7 was only a few hours away, and I was determined not to be watching it tonight in a Ramada. And not with these guys!

I could have flown into New York City, headed for Yankee Stadium, and blown the cash I had just made from the corporate gig on a lousy single seat. but that was really out of the question. The last place I wanted to be if things went badly was the Bronx.

I'm gonna enjoy this game from the comfort of my living room, where I can absolutely guarantee there will be no Yankees fans. There is no way, win or lose, that I'll have this evening spoiled by an obnoxious Yankees fan.

So I flew back to Boston and was a few miles from home when the cell rang.

It was Tony V., a friend and fellow comedian (go see him, he's one of the best!).

Tony was in L.A. and was scheduled to appear on *Jimmy Kimmel Live* the following evening. Knowing he was from Boston, the producers asked if he knew any die-hard Sox fans who would like to debate some Yankees after the game.

"How quickly can you get to Fenway?"

"Forty-five minutes."

"Make sure you're wearing a Sox shirt."

"Already wearing one."

"Go."

"I'm gone."

Next thing you know, I was back at Fenway, sitting on the sidewalk, watching the game with a couple of dozen fans on a small TV the camera crew had rigged up.

They wired me up with a mike and earplug and soon I would be talking live to one of the funniest guys on TV! Live!

Cheers echoed down Landsdowne Street, from the packed bars and nightclubs in the shadow of the Green Monster as Johnny Damon and the boys roughed up Kevin Brown for an early lead.

By the time we went to air, the outcome was obvious. The Sox were poised to complete the greatest comeback in baseball history.

"How are things up there in Boston?" Jimmy Kimmel asked, via satellite.

"How are things going?" I responded. "We're going to the World Series, man! Tonight's gonna be the mother of all parties! It's gonna be insane. We may even defrost Ted Williams for this one!"

Dozens of Sox fans behind me began the obligatory "Yankees suck!" chant.

I've participated in many—and this was by far the sweetest!

"So what's gonna happen up there tonight?" asked Jimmy.

"We're gonna get drunk and flip over any car we find that has New York plates!" I joked.

More chants!

Jimmy then went to a bar in New York and spoke with some devastated Yankees fans.

He wanted to check back with us later, when the outcome became official, but the Boston cops had other plans.

They wanted us out—now. Something about permits. Public nuisance. Whatever. They just wanted us out.

A few minutes later, the crew sent back its last broadcast to L.A. for the evening, a quick shot of the cops leading us out of the area.

"Apparently there is a riot being planned up in Boston and our crew has been told to leave," Jimmy joked.

We were both just kidding around. I'm pretty sure neither of us expected what was coming next.

DANCING IN THE STREETS

You hear the expression "dancing in the streets" all the time. But have you ever actually seen people dancing in the streets? In Boston?

Well, tonight we danced like MC Hammer with a bee in his pants.

I've been to some pretty wild parties in my day, but nothing compares to what I saw in Boston tonight.

Not what you saw on TV. They'll show that stuff for days, looping the same footage of a couple of cars that were torched and some drunken a-holes breaking windows.

That's not the real story. For the real story, you had to be in the streets . . . dancing.

If you weren't there, I'm not sure anyone could describe it to you. I know I can't.

I can describe this, though, about the funniest thing I've ever seen. A buck naked man with a bottle of champagne dancing down Mass. Ave. and hugging all takers. And he got more hugs than Wally on Kids Day!

The city's traffic was gridlocked for hours as people just parked in the middle of streets and partied on their hoods.

Dancing in the streets!

The dancing lasted through the morning, a wild night of jubilation and intoxication.

They say New York is the city that never sleeps, but I guarantee they were tucked in bed early tonight.

Sleep tight, Yankees fans.

We're gonna stay up for a while and celebrate the greatest comeback in baseball history!

FLY-BY

Following the opening ceremonies of game 1 of the World Series, moments after Steven Tyler rocked the last notes of the national anthem, the Fenway faithful were treated to a fly-by from the Vermont Air National Guard, aka The Green Mountain Boys.

I love the fly-by. It's the ultimate show of military bravado. Before we play, we flex our muscles for all to see with a demonstration of our most impressive weapons.

The fly-by says to the world . . .

We're gonna play some baseball for a while and just in case you were thinking of screwing with us, have you seen our shiny new F-16 Falcon fighters?

This is an American thing that only the mighty U.S. of A. can pull off.

I can't picture any other nation attempting a similar display of military prowess.

Imagine, in Afghanistan, rake-wielding rebel fighters in synchronized formation, crossing a dusty soccer field on their swiftest donkeys.

Or in France, right before the championship croquet match, a guy in a suit circles the wickets waving a multilateral treaty.

I don't think that Steven Tyler would open for that gig.

IT'S OVER.

Still in disbelief, and emotionally and physically exhausted from weeks of late-night baseball drama, I stared at the television, watching every bit of the World Series celebration coverage.

Then, as if he was talking to me directly, I heard Jason Varitek tell a reporter, "I'm just happy that the people in New England can now sleep at night."

Good idea, Tek. I'm going to bed.

But I'm gonna bundle up first, because if my dad is right, Hell will be frozen over by morning.

SPECIAL THANKS TO:

Tom Caron, Peter Frechette, Jim Carroll, Butch Sterns,

Steve Sera, John Martin, Pat Gamere, Eric Sharmer,
Chris Del Dotto, Chris Heinze, Sarge, Eric Freede, Sam Horn
and everyone at NESN

Peter, Deidre, and Grace at Peter E. Randall Publishing

Kevin "Lucky" Mealey, Marcos Rey, George Hamm,
Larry Trinceri, Budd Perry, Gary and Julie Marino, Oliver
Keithly, Sarah Dearing, my friends at Olympia Sports,
Portsmouth Magazine, Dee Mura, Scotty and Richard at CREA,
Mike Quinn, Curtis International, Dot O'Donnell, Rubyhorse,
Greg and the Morning Buzz, everyone at the Comedy Connec-
tion in Boston, Ron, Michael, Matt and Brian up on the roof,
Johnny Tobin, The Sons of Sam Horn, Susan Carter
Photography, Jen Sharron, Elfie, Lenny Clarke, Mike Clarke,
Don Gavin, Matty Blake, Rich Ceisler, P.J. Thibideau,

Tony V., The Viper, and Kevin Knox for the
funniest 24 hrs of my life.

Jay Miller and the gang at the Courtyard, Paulie at the garage
for keeping an eye on the "rocket car" all summer, the boys at
Port City for introducing me to the "rocket car,"

Ma, Sue, Riley Joe, Julia, Joe Carter, Coach Dunn, Jenna, Gabby,
Lulu and Mad Mags,

T$ and Q-man for keeping me young and immature.

And of course, Judie.

About the Author

Jimmy Dunn is a professional
stand-up comedian and lifelong Sox fan.
He lives with his dog, Buckner.

photo: Marc Page, Portsmouth Magazine